A WAGGERS TALE

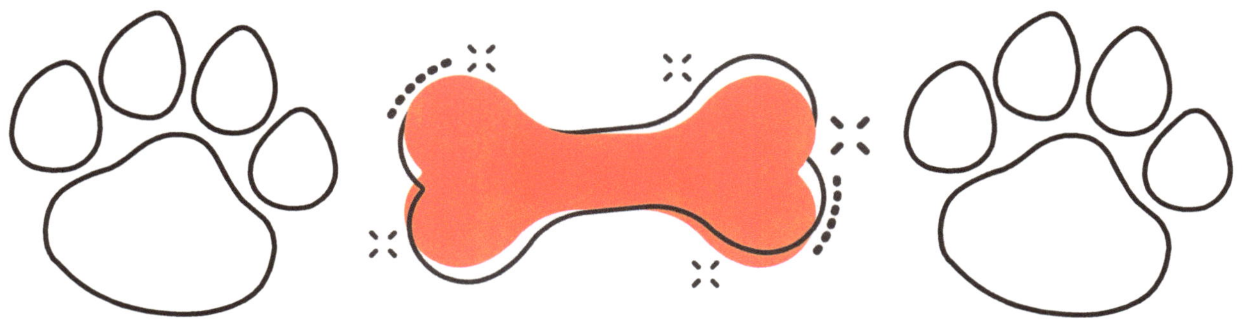

TOLD THROUGH THE EYES OF A RESCUE

Written and Illustrated

By

LaNell Forrest

ISBN 979-8-89130-312-6 (paperback)
ISBN 978-1-63874-949-3 (hardcover)
ISBN 978-1-63874-950-9 (digital)

Christian Faith Publishing
832 Park Avenue
Meadville, PA 16335
www.christianfaithpublishing.com

Printed in the United States of America

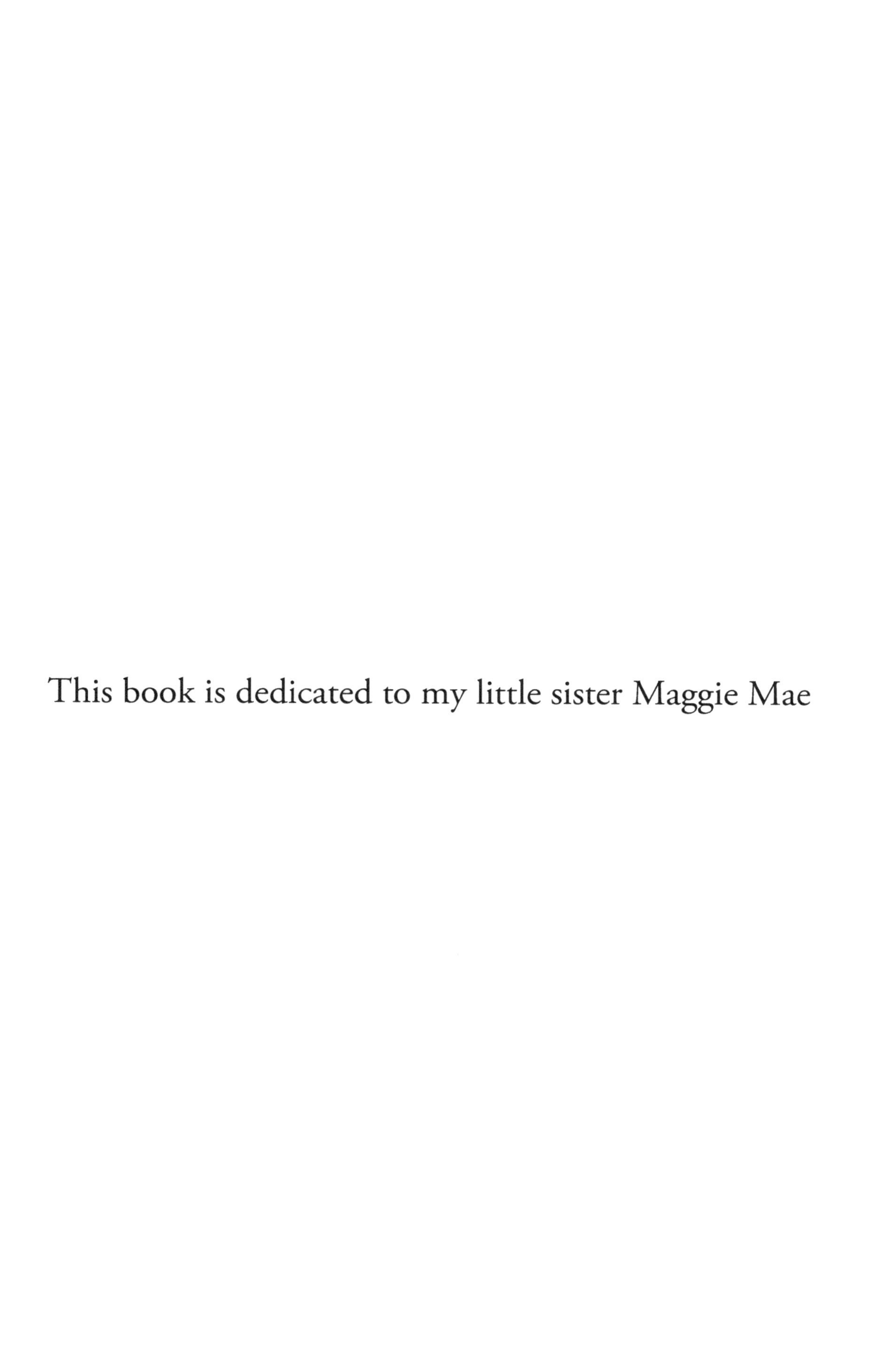

This book is dedicated to my little sister Maggie Mae

My name is
Moby Dickerson
and
this is My Story.

ROAD TRIP

I lived with my foster mommy and daddy until my new mommy and daddy adopted me.

My new mommy took me
on a long trip to my new home
to meet my new daddy.

I left North Carolina
and moved south to
become a

'BEACH DOGGIE'!

I was scared to leave my foster parents. Getting used to my new home was hard. I missed my foster mommy and daddy. I tried to run away a lot but was always caught.

After a while, I decided to stay because my new mommy and daddy loved me. I thought this is okay, and I was beginning to love them too!

best friends
forever!

Mommy took me shopping for toys. She gave me a choice of three toys. I picked out a whale! I thought, if I was named after the whale Moby Dick, then I needed this toy whale. He is my best buddy!

This was great! A new home, new mommy and daddy, and a new best buddy. My whale! I decided then I was never going to run away again.

I had a lot to get used to. I didn't think that there would be times when I would be left alone while Mommy and Daddy went on errands.

When Daddy left to run errands, I would stand at the window waiting for him to come back home. I don't like it when Mommy and Daddy leave me.

Just as I was getting used to my new home and loving it, my mommy started putting clothes on me! I didn't know she loved doggie clothes. And that's not all.

She started making me wear sunglasses too! Oh my good-
ness and a hat! Now I was beginning to wonder if I had made a
big mistake. Oh well, I just went along with Mommy, because
I was so loved and my new life was awesome.

One day, it was just Daddy and me at home. Mommy was gone all day. I got into big trouble! Daddy and I were outside near the pond. I saw a big bird on the bank. I wanted that bird, so I ran after it. As it flew away over the pond, so did I! I landed right in that pond, but quickly got out.

Daddy screamed, "You're in Big Trouble now, Buddy!"

When Mommy got home, she was so mad. She took me right in and made me take a bath. *Yuck!*

We were getting along just fine, and I had Mommy and Daddy just where I wanted them…*under my paws!* All of a sudden, I got a little sister. It was very quick, and I was not a happy puppy.

Her name is Maggie Mae. I didn't know what to think at first, but I quickly had to accept she wasn't going to leave.

ITS HARD TO SHARE!

Talk about Trouble. We didn't like each other at first, because we had to learn to share Mommy and Daddy. After a while, we got to know each other, so I decided she wasn't so bad after all.

We love each other now, even though she became quite "bossy" and tried to take over. I started standing up for myself and let her know that this was my home too! Now, I just ignore her being so bossy.

Maggie Mae had to quickly fall in line like me when Mommy started dressing her too. That only made her "prissy" *and* "bossy." Oh boy! She thought she was something, and in no time, she became "Daddy's little girl." Oh well, Mommy is all mine! "Mommy's little boy.'"

JUST CALL ME Princess

Maggie thinks she is a Princess and needs a tiara. Really, Maggie? She's living in her fairy tale world. She can be a real pest sometimes, but I love her anyway.

Soap
Hygiene
and
Hair care
items.
Tooth
paste

Now came more rules Mommy made for both of us. We begin our day by eating breakfast, getting our faces washed, teeth brushed, and hair combed. Next comes getting dressed for the day. What a pain, but then we get our treats. We have to work for our treats! Then our day finally begins.

I like to play ball and tease Mommy with my whale. We play
Tug of War with my best buddy, the whale.

Maggie has a favorite toy too! She plays Tug of War with Daddy and her rabbit.

24

Her bedtime toy is her Duckie. We both love our toys, and Maggie knows not to get near my whale, and I leave her rabbit and duckie alone too.

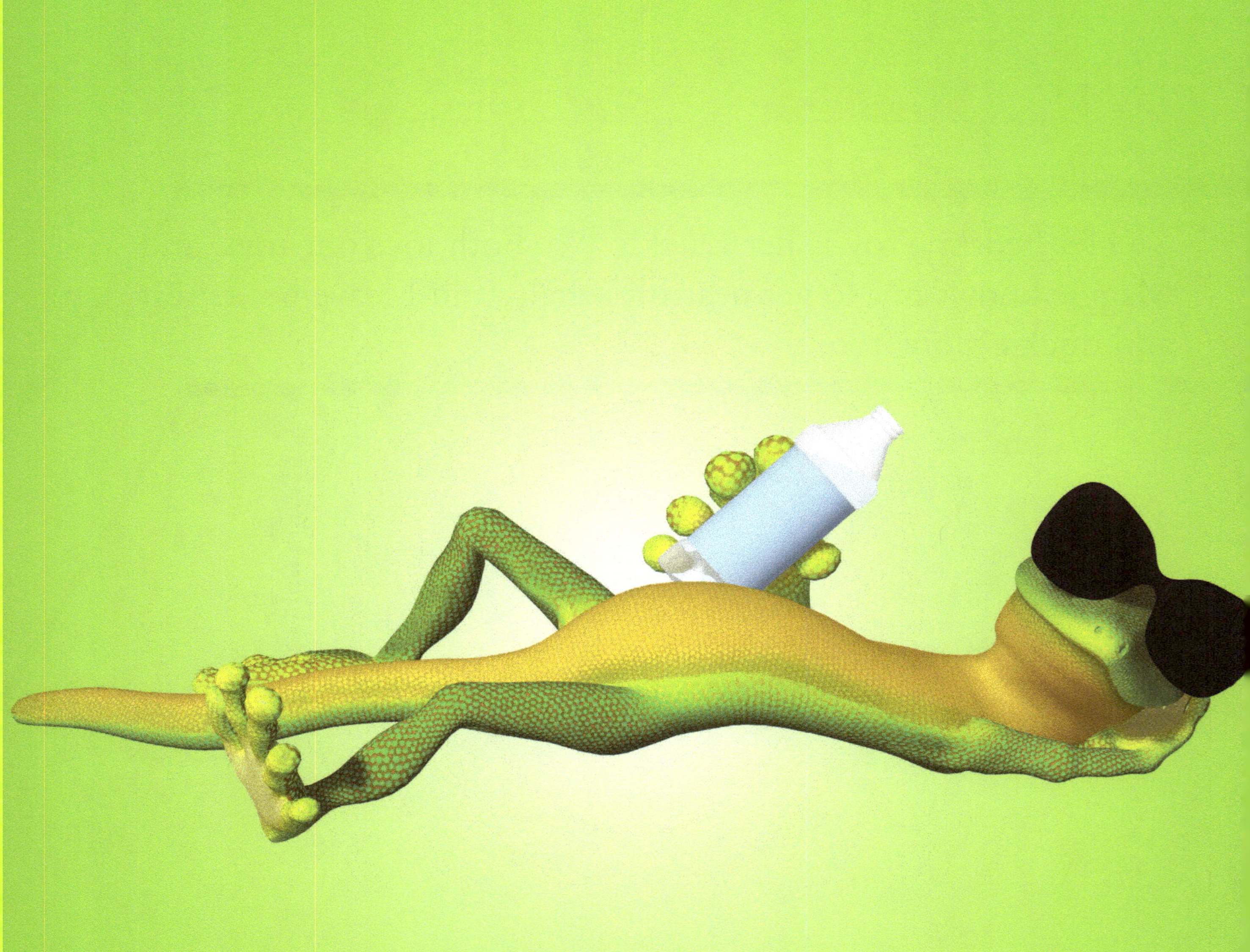

In the summer, I like to search for Geckos on the patio. They know how to hide from me, but I will get me one someday!

Maggie just likes to lay in the sun and take a sunbath. She's the Princess you know!

Maggie and I have had many adventures and know there are more to come. Our lives are awesome. We are so lucky to have been adopted by our Mommy and Daddy. We love them, and they love us. When you are loved so much and taken care of so well, you should do everything to be good. When you do this, you will be loved in a special way always—just like Maggie and me.

ABOUT THE AUTHOR

LaNell Forrest is a native of North Carolina. She is a graduate of Wake Forest University with a BA in Art and an Associate of Applied Science: Dental Hygiene Degree from Central Piedmont Community College. Always having a soft heart for canines, she has, in recent years, turned her heart to rescue canines. She currently resides in Georgia, with a friend and her two rescue puppies.